SAVING A SYSTEM IN PERIL

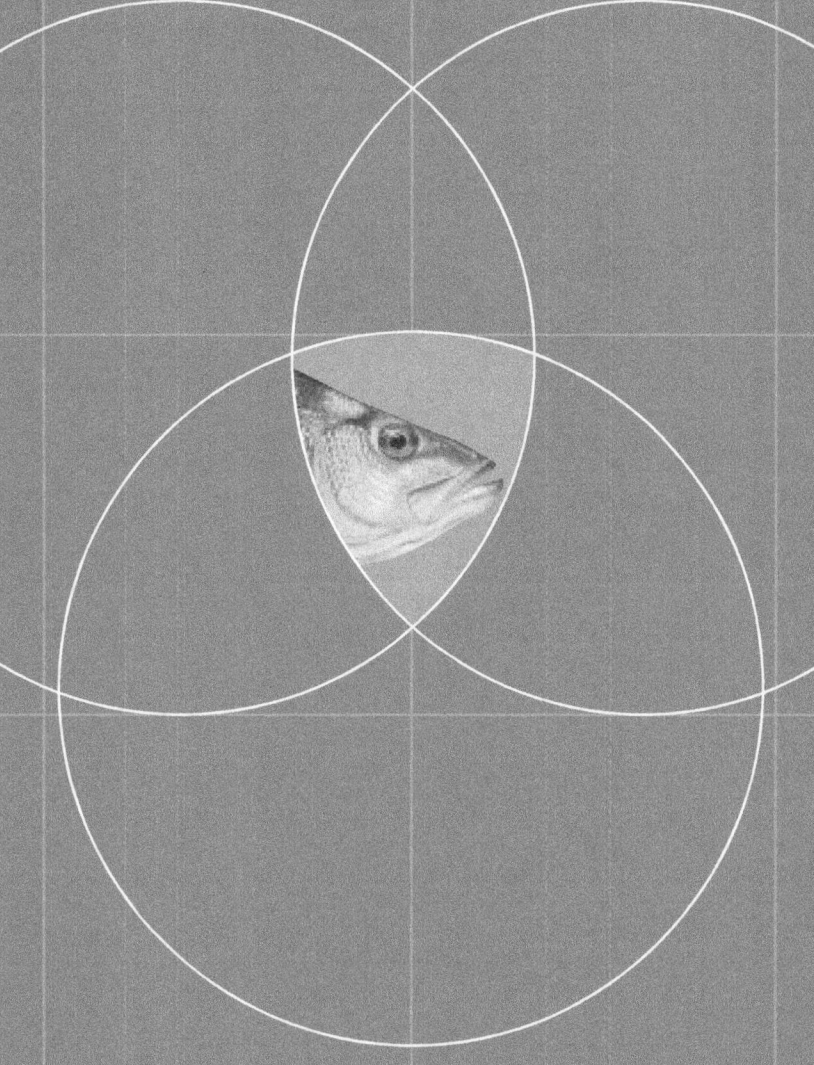

A SPECIAL REPORT ON THE
NATIONAL FISH HATCHERY SYSTEM
BY THE SPORT FISHING AND BOATING
PARTNERSHIP COUNCIL SEPTEMBER 2000

A note about the cover: The 20 squares on the front depict the 20 recommendations contained in the report, while the intersecting circles, with the fish at the nexus, represent the consensus reached by the wide variety of stakeholders involved in the project.

CONTENTS

THE SPORT FISHING AND BOATING PARTNERSHIP COUNCIL (SFBPC) serves as a unique adviser to the Secretary of the Interior and the Director of the U.S. Fish and Wildlife Service. The Council, formed in January 1993, represents the interests of the public and private sectors of the sport fishing and boating communities and is organized to enhance partnerships among industry, constituency groups and government.

The Council is chartered under the Federal Advisory Committee Act. Its membership of up to 18 people includes the director of the Fish and Wildlife Service and the president of the International Association of Fish and Wildlife Agencies, who both serve in ex officio capacities. Other Council members are directors from state agencies responsible for managing recreational fish and wildlife resources and individuals who represent the interests of saltwater and freshwater recreational fishing, recreational boating, the recreational fishing and boating industries, recreational fisheries resources conservation, aquatic resource outreach and education, and tourism.

More information about the SFBPC can be found on the Internet at http://sfbpc.fws.gov or by contacting the Council's offices at 703/358 1711.

SPORT FISHING AND BOATING PARTNERSHIP COUNCIL (SFBPC) MEMBERS

COUNCIL CHAIR
Helen Sevier
Chief Executive Officer
Bass Anglers Sportsman Society
(B.A.S.S. Inc.)

James Anderson
Executive Director
Northwest Indian Fisheries Commission

Tom Bedell
Chairman and Chief Executive Officer
Pure Fishing

Jamie Clark (ex officio)
Director
U.S. Fish and Wildlife Service

Doug Hansen
Director
Division of Wildlife
South Dakota Department of
Game, Fish and Parks

Paul Hansen
Executive Director
Izaak Walton League of America

Charles Harter III
Board of Directors
Coastal Conservation Association

Mike Hough
President
States Organization for Boating Access

Jim Kalkofen
Executive Director
Professional Walleye Trail

Barbara Knuth
Associate Professor
Natural Resource Policy and Management
Cornell University

Ryck Lydecker
Associate Director for State Affairs
BOAT/U.S.

Robert McDowell
Director
New Jersey Division of Fish, Game
and Wildlife

Alfred Russo
Business Unit Manager/Director
Stren Fishing Lines Division
Remington Arms Co. Inc.

Eddie Smith
Chairman and Chief Executive Officer
Grady-White Boats Inc.

William Taylor
Vice Provost and Dean
Michigan State University
College of Agriculture and
Natural Resources

David Waller (ex officio)
President
International Association of Fish
and Wildlife Agencies

Director
Wildlife Resources Division
Georgia Department of Natural Resources

Carl Wilgus
Administrator
Division of Tourism
Idaho Department of Commerce

SFBPC NATIONAL FISH HATCHERY PROJECT STEERING COMMITTEE

MEMBERSHIP AND REPRESENTATION

The National Fish Hatchery Project Steering Committee was assembled by the Technical Working Group of the Sport Fishing and Boating Partnership Council in the latter months of 1999 and the early months of 2000.

Each person on the steering committee served in his capacity as an individual fisheries professional. It is important to note that these individuals have served the fisheries community for a number of years and have represented many fisheries interest groups during their careers. Their breadth and depth of knowledge of a diverse array of fisheries management issues and constituents' perspectives were extremely beneficial to this project.

The following list contains the name of each steering committee participant, accompanied by the name of the participant's employer or the interest group with which the participant is affiliated. The listing of these organizations does not imply endorsement of this report by these groups. Rather, these organizations are listed to provide context for the report by illustrating the diversity of experience and philosophies that came into play during the report's creation. It should be noted that the organizations on this list recognized the importance of this report by essentially donating the time each steering committee member invested in this process.

SFBPC NATIONAL FISH HATCHERY PROJECT STEERING COMMITTEE MEMBERS

Gary Myers
Executive Director
Tennessee Wildlife Resources Agency
Representative
International Association of Fish
and Wildlife Agencies

Jim Range
Representative
American Fly Fishing Trade Association

Bruce Shupp
National Conservation Director
Bass Anglers Sportsman Society
(B.A.S.S. Inc.)

Stephen Smith
National Marine Fisheries Service (retired)

Bruce Suzumoto
Manager
Special Projects
Northwest Power Planning Council

Whitney Tilt
Director of Conservation
National Fish and Wildlife Foundation

Robert Wiley
Section Manager
Fisheries Management
Wyoming Game and Fish Department

NATIONAL FISH HATCHERY
PROJECT MANAGER
Noreen Clough
President
NKC Environmental Consulting Inc.

STEERING COMMITTEE MEETING FACILITATORS
Barb Springer Beck
President
Beck Consulting

John Mundinger
Proprietor
Consulting for Creative Solutions

SPORT FISHING AND BOATING PARTNERSHIP
COUNCIL COORDINATOR
Laury Parramore

EXECUTIVE SUMMARY

For more than a century, the National Fish Hatchery System (NFHS) has played a valuable role in providing cultured fish to benefit Americans. The Department of the Interior's U.S. Fish and Wildlife Service (FWS) manages the system, consisting of 66 national fish hatcheries, seven fish technology centers, and nine fish health centers.

Unfortunately, the NFHS has serious problems that have developed over several decades. Funding for hatchery operations and maintenance has declined by about 15 percent since 1992. NFHS facilities are old and outmoded. As a whole, the system suffers from a maintenance backlog of approximately $300 million. Twenty-five percent of hatchery personnel positions are vacant. To a troubling degree, these problems reflect an erosion of congressional and public support.

In March 1999, U.S. Representative George Miller, of the House Committee on Resources, asked the General Accounting Office (GAO) to conduct a review to evaluate the NFHS and to gauge the need for changes to refine and clarify the system's legal mandates. In May 1999, 10 members of Congress requested that the FWS begin a process to determine the role and mission of the NFHS. In August 1999, the FWS asked the federally chartered Sport Fishing and Boating Partnership Council (SFBPC) to undertake that review. Following the FWS request, the SFBPC convened a special National Fish Hatchery Project Steering Committee to review the NFHS and develop recommendations regarding the system's roles, responsibilities and strategic funding policies.

Overall, the steering committee believes the NFHS is uniquely positioned to influence and benefit state and tribal fishery programs, fulfill tribal trust responsibilities, and provide technical assistance to private aquaculture. Although the intent of the steering committee's report is to provide recommendations for future management of the NFHS, the steering committee concluded that without a national vision to define regional goals and objectives designed to fulfill overall FWS Fisheries Program strategies, the national hatchery system will continue to drift and will be in peril. It is essential that the FWS move aggressively to ensure that the NFHS and the products it produces fit within a publicly reviewed national strategy developed with state and tribal partners and stakeholders. The FWS must commit to implementing the plan it produces, and the FWS, the administration and Congress must be prepared to fund adequately the activities outlined by this plan.

"Forty million anglers will be watching to see if Congress and the U.S. Fish and Wildlife Service will respond to these consensus recommendations."
–JIM MARTIN, CONSERVATION DIRECTOR, PURE FISHING

In addition to its observation regarding the need for a Fisheries Program national strategy, the steering committee's review resulted in 20 consensus-based recommendations, presented without priority, in the programmatic categories of Scientific Excellence and Accountability, Mitigation, Recreation and Other Cooperative Programs, Threatened and Endangered Species Recovery, and Native Species Restoration.

The steering committee's recommendations acknowledge the NFHS' vital roles in meeting federal mitigation obligations, restoring and maintaining native fisheries, and participating in the recovery of threatened and endangered aquatic species. The recommendations also urge the FWS and the NFHS to strengthen cooperative efforts with states, tribes and partners and improve accountability with Congress, stakeholders and the general public.

A repeated theme in the report is the requirement to produce and use cultured products from the NFHS in conformance with the best possible science-based management principles and practices. The recommendations emphasize the crucial role fish technology centers, fish health centers and the national brood-stock programs play in ensuring these principles and practices are followed.

The report acknowledges the NFHS' role in providing fish to mitigate the impact of federal development activities and asks for legislative clarification of that responsibility and authority for full cost recovery for mitigation-related expenses from the parties responsible for development projects. The report also recommends that Congress clarify the role the NFHS should play in supporting recreational fishing objectives beyond the current benefits provided by mitigation and restoration activities.

Work on national fish hatcheries in support of threatened and endangered species recovery is affirmed by the steering committee as an appropriate and important use. However, the steering committee recommends that in the future this work be funded by threatened and endangered species program appropriations.

The long-term stability of the NFHS will be solidified further by implementing the steering committee's recommendations that acknowledge the system's significant role in the restoration of native fisheries.

Finally, the steering committee recommends the FWS work closely with affected tribes to ensure that the responsibilities of the NFHS, with regard to tribal trust and treaty agreements, are clarified and properly implemented.

As a result of the review, the steering committee concluded that it is imperative that the FWS position its Fisheries Program and the NFHS to provide federal leadership in development and application of the best possible fish culture and fisheries management practices. The steering committee based its review on what it believes are overriding considerations for fisheries conservation and management: the maintenance of healthy wild fish populations through habitat conservation and improved harvest management, maintenance of genetic diversity, and the proper use of hatchery stocks in achieving fishery management objectives.

When implemented, the steering committee's recommendations will clarify the role of and expectations for the NFHS and will result in substantial changes to its direction and management.

SPORT FISHING AND BOATING PARTNERSHIP COUNCIL

INTRODUCTION

For more than a century, the National Fish Hatchery System (NFHS) has played a valuable role in providing a variety of cultured fish to benefit the American people. The Department of the Interior's U.S. Fish and Wildlife Service (FWS) manages the system, which presently consists of 82 facilities—66 national fish hatcheries, seven fish technology centers, and nine fish health centers.

Unfortunately, the NFHS has serious problems. Due to the increasing diversity and complexity of their responsibilities, these facilities do not operate as a true system. The role of national fish hatcheries in aquatic resource management programs is unclear and controversial. Funding deficits are legend. The U.S. Congress, the FWS, other federal and state agencies, tribes and stakeholders, including conservation organizations and members of the angling community, agree that fundamental changes are needed if the NFHS is to be effective in the 21st century. This report provides resource managers and decision-makers with a series of recommendations that will refocus and revitalize the NFHS and enable it to realize its fullest potential as a tool in aquatic resource management.

The NFHS' problems developed over several decades. Internal and external pressures led to differing opinions and confusion about the system's primary objectives and the principal products it should provide. Increased pressure on fisheries resources, increased knowledge of fisheries management, growth in the capabilities of state and tribal partners, and criticism of hatcheries for past practices all are factors causing the system's role to become unclear. The FWS' priorities for its hatcheries also have shifted in recent years away from the traditional role of stocking fish to meet recreational angling demand to a greater role in native fish recovery and restoration. These rapidly changing priorities, failure to implement past FWS Fishery Program plans, and insufficient communication with partners and stakeholders have further affected the system. In turn, congressional and public support for the system has eroded.

This erosion of support is evidenced by declining funding and support from Congress and the administration. Although the FWS' overall budget rose 35 percent since 1992 (in constant 1999 dollars), funding for hatchery operations and maintenance declined by about 15 percent, forcing the FWS to narrow hatchery objectives and reduce hatchery system planning, monitoring and evaluation. NFHS facilities now average 55 years in age, and much of the infrastructure is outmoded. There is an estimated $300 million maintenance backlog. Twenty-five percent of hatchery personnel positions are vacant.

"Hatcheries are an important tool for natural resource managers when properly selected and used in support of habitat protection and fisheries management. We need to keep this tool sharp, focused and effective."

—WHITNEY TILT, DIRECTOR OF CONSERVATION, NATIONAL FISH AND WILDLIFE FOUNDATION

On March 18, 1999, U.S. Representative George Miller, of the House Committee on Resources, asked the General Accounting Office (GAO) to conduct a review to serve as a baseline for evaluating the NFHS and for gauging the need for changes in existing law to refine and clarify the system's legal mandates (Attachment 1). On May 26, 1999, 10 members of Congress requested that FWS begin an open, inclusive and participatory process to determine the role and overall mission of the NFHS (Attachment 2). In August 1999, the FWS asked the federally chartered Sport Fishing and Boating Partnership Council (SFBPC) to undertake the review (Attachments 3 and 4).

Following the FWS' request, the SFBPC convened a special National Fish Hatchery Project Steering Committee. The steering committee's mission was to conduct a broad and balanced review of the NFHS and from that review develop consensus-based positions and recommendations about the roles, responsibilities and strategic funding policies for the system, within the broader fisheries management role of the FWS.

EVALUATION

Members of the SFBPC National Fish Hatchery Project Steering Committee represent federal, state and tribal fishery resource managers and fish culturists, academia, aquaculture and members of the conservation and sport fishing communities. Members initially were chosen from or by the SFBPC's Technical Working Group, which consists of state, federal, tribal, conservation organization and industry representatives. The steering committee then was supplemented with other individuals to ensure a wide diversity of viewpoints.

Despite the participation of tribal representatives, the steering committee was forced to conclude that it did not have sufficient background or expertise to adequately define the NFHS' role with regard to tribal trust obligations. Although references to tribal trust responsibilities occur throughout this report, the steering committee believes these references may not adequately address the NFHS' complete trust responsibility.

However, it is clear from the steering committee's investigations that the tribes would like the FWS to take a more holistic view of the NFHS' role in aquatic resource management. The tribes believe national fish hatcheries should provide fish to enhance tribal fisheries programs and to help tribes conserve and rebuild stocks and mitigate for past activities that have damaged naturally occurring populations.

The products of the FWS' National Fish Hatchery Tribal Working Group hopefully will help the NFHS define its tribal trust responsibilities. The FWS also has a Native American policy to provide additional context. Further, important trust responsibilities are articulated in the Secretarial Order on American Indian Tribal Rights and the Federal-Tribal Trust Responsibilities and the Endangered Species Act.

The steering committee began by examining the congressional directives calling for this review, identifying steering committee members' concerns, evaluating the current state of the NFHS, and gathering and analyzing information available in a variety of reports. The latter include the October 1999 GAO report "National Fish Hatcheries—Classification of the Distribution of Fish and Fish Eggs Needs Refinement" and the June 2000 GAO report "National Fish Hatcheries: Authority Needed to Better Align Operations With Priorities." The steering committee also consulted actively with the FWS and reviewed the FWS Hatchery System Alignment report.

"It was truly inspiring to watch seasoned professionals from across the spectrum of opinion on the roles and appropriate uses of cultured fish reach consensus around a set of forward-looking recommendations to stabilize and reform the National Fish Hatchery System."

—NORVILLE PROSSER, STEERING COMMITTEE CHAIRMAN, VICE PRESIDENT, AMERICAN SPORTFISHING ASSOCIATION

Throughout the years, the NFHS has been the subject of numerous other studies, reports and recommendations from conservation groups, committees appointed by the FWS, and a variety of task forces. Attachment 5 provides a brief summary of four major reports and a compilation of their recommendations, which the steering committee considered as important references. In addition, the steering committee identified new ideas, issues and changing scientific perspectives about the production and use of hatchery fish that have emerged since the previous reports were published.

The steering committee believes the NFHS is uniquely positioned to influence and benefit state and tribal fisheries programs, fulfill tribal trust responsibilities, and provide technical assistance to private aquaculture. However, these expectations have not been achieved to date because the FWS has not developed and implemented a clearly understood and publicly accepted strategy for its Fisheries Program. A vision for the NFHS must fall within such a strategy that outlines the NFHS' role in fisheries management, including genetics and brood-stock management, scientific advances in fish production, fish health and fish technology development, and post-production and post-stocking monitoring.

Although the intent of this document is to provide recommendations for future management of the NFHS, the steering committee concluded that without a national vision to define regional goals and objectives designed to fulfill overall Fisheries Program strategies, the national hatchery system will continue to drift and will be in peril. It is essential that the FWS move aggressively to ensure that the NFHS and the products it produces fit within a publicly reviewed, national strategy developed with state and tribal partners and stakeholders, using a process similar to the development of the FWS' "Action Plan for Fisheries and Aquatic Resources." Unlike the action plan, however, the FWS must commit to implementing the plan it produces, and the FWS, the administration and Congress must be prepared to fund adequately the activities outlined by this plan.

Nevertheless, the recommendations presented below must be implemented regardless of the existence of a national vision for the FWS Fisheries Program. The steering committee believes it would be beneficial for the FWS to adopt and implement these recommendations as soon as possible to begin the process of reversing the downward slide of the NFHS. Implementation cannot await completion of national visions or strategic plans; rather, those visions and plans should reflect and embody the steering committee's recommendations to the maximum extent possible.

ROLES, RESPONSIBILITIES, AND OPERATION OF THE NATIONAL FISH HATCHERY SYSTEM

It is imperative that the FWS position its Fisheries Program and the NFHS to provide federal leadership in the development and application of the best possible fish culture and fisheries management practices. In advancing these ideals, the steering committee believes the overriding considerations for fisheries conservation and management are maintaining healthy wild populations through habitat conservation and improved harvest management, maintaining genetic diversity, and properly using hatchery stocks to achieve fishery objectives. Decisions to stock cultured fish should derive from a broad need, based on ecologically, economically and socially responsible aquatic resource management. Current fisheries management theory and science recognize that hatchery fish are only part of the solution to declining fishery resources.

The steering committee's recommendations are arranged in the following categories and are numbered sequentially. The numbering of the recommendations does not indicate a priority order. In keeping with the guidelines established at the steering committee's first meeting in December 1999, the recommendations are consensus-based and presented by programmatic categories, without priority.

Scientific Excellence and Accountability

Mitigation

Recreation and Other Cooperative Programs

Threatened and Endangered Species Recovery

Native Species Restoration

When implemented, the steering committee's findings and recommendations will result in substantial changes to the direction of the NFHS and the way it is managed by the FWS.

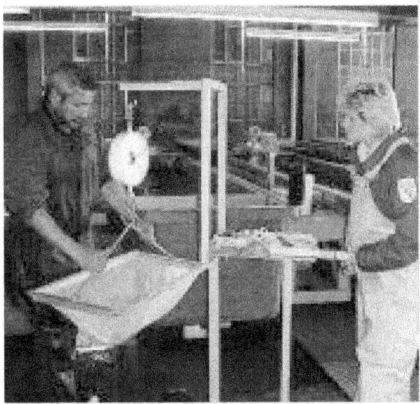

RECOMMENDATIONS

SCIENTIFIC EXCELLENCE AND ACCOUNTABILITY

1 The FWS and its cooperators must develop and adhere to resource-specific, scientifically based fishery management plans. Plans must relate to national and regional fisheries goals and objectives calling for use of NFHS fish in programs for restoration, recovery, mitigation, tribal trust responsibilities or recreation on federal lands. Requests for NFHS fish will result from needs as described in these plans.

Fish from the NFHS must be used in ways defined in and guided by management plans that identify goals and objectives for stocked fish and post-stocking criteria to measure their success. The steering committee was unaware of any overall guidance document or strategic plan that matches national fish hatchery production objectives with a series of national, regional and local management plans and production requests. Fish will not be made available if no such plan exists.

The steering committee knows the FWS is waiting for this report before beginning a strategic planning process for the NFHS. However, planning for the NFHS must not be done in isolation but must be predicated on a national strategy and regional goals and objectives for the FWS' overall Fisheries Program—one developed with stakeholders and one that balances habitat conservation, restoration and fisheries management with a strategy for use of hatchery-produced fish. The steering committee expects the FWS to use the recommendations in this report as an important component of the planning process for the NFHS.

2 NFHS facilities (including fish technology centers, fish health centers and brood-stock hatcheries) must develop and adhere to operational work plans describing the purpose and function of each unit. Work plans must relate to national and regional fisheries goals and objectives and be updated every two years. At the end of each fiscal year, a performance report must be prepared, detailing how the operational work plans are being implemented. These reports will be submitted by the regions to FWS headquarters, which will subsequently forward a compilation of highlights to appropriate congressional committees, state and tribal managers, and other stakeholders.

Operational plans should be scientifically based with production objectives tied to specific, approved management or recovery plans. Plans should address operational and genetic protocols, fish health hazards and risks, on-site product performance, and post-production and post-stocking monitoring.

3 To enhance program understanding and ensure program integrity and accountability, FWS must report to Congress biennially on the status of the activities of the NFHS and how they relate to national and regional fisheries goals and objectives. Reports will include the complete costs of producing fish, as well as the numbers and performance of fish produced, the program for which they were produced (e.g. mitigation, recreation, restoration or recovery) and their overall contribution to fisheries and aquatic ecosystem recovery and/or conservation. Draft reports will be made available to the SFBPC and to partners and stakeholders for review and comment, and a final report incorporating partner/stakeholder review presented to Congress, the Council, and the public. The first draft report should be available not later than July 1, 2002, and every other year thereafter.

Reporting is at the very heart of accountability and is essential to rebuilding congressional confidence in the NFHS. Biennial reports that are reviewed by partners and stakeholders and then presented to Congress and the public provide an important programmatic audit now missing for the NFHS. Currently, the difference between actual production costs and administrative costs is not known. Consequently, this reporting also may be important in determining the cost-effectiveness of FWS activities as compared to activities undertaken by partners.

> *"This report, done by extremely qualified and very committed professionals, is an excellent guideline to be followed in saving and even enhancing the very important National Fish Hatchery System."*
>
> —EDDIE SMITH, CHIEF EXECUTIVE OFFICER, GRADY-WHITE BOATS

4 FWS must develop jointly with tribes a separate, clearly defined strategy outlining how the NFHS will meet its tribal trust responsibilities.

As a result of the steering committee's deliberations, it became abundantly clear that few, if any, individuals within or outside the FWS precisely understand the agency's tribal trust responsibilities as they relate to the goals, objectives and operations of the NFHS. The FWS National Fish Hatchery Tribal Working Group is developing a report that should help inform this process.

5 FWS and its partners should consider and use as appropriate the 1995 American Fisheries Society publication "Use and Effects of Cultured Fishes in Aquatic Ecosystems" in preparing management and operational plans.

This publication provides a number of valuable considerations for fisheries managers who are preparing to use captively propagated aquatic species to achieve fishery (or other aquatic wildlife) management objectives.

6 Post-stocking evaluations must be conducted and documented regularly to determine the quality of the fish stocked, impacts on natural populations, and how well they achieve the specific goals and objectives for which they were stocked, as defined in a fishery management or recovery plan.

Requirements for monitoring and evaluation should be developed cooperatively by the FWS and state, tribal and other federal fisheries managers to ensure evaluations are useful for measuring fishery goals while also being timely and fiscally efficient. As a part of the need for accountability, the evaluations should be documented and be available to partners and interested parties upon request.

7 Activities and products of the NFHS' fish technology and fish health centers and national brood-stock program facilities should be defined by recommendations resulting from a needs assessment involving partners and stakeholders. Operational work plans described in Recommendation 2 will be designed to meet these needs. Likewise, the FWS must focus funding for operations and maintenance of these facilities based on the needs identified.

Fish health centers, fish technology centers and the national brood-stock program must be recognized as a high priority for the FWS and must be funded accordingly. These facilities are important contributors to maintaining healthy fisheries and aquatic ecosystems, as described in Attachment 6. The importance of fish health and fish technology centers and the brood-stock program and the demand for their services and for the improved quality (genetics and health) of hatchery-reared fish far exceed current funding and staffing.

The steering committee is concerned that these facilities are not fulfilling the integral role they play in the NFHS. These facilities also are not realizing their potential to provide the best science possible to national fish hatcheries, state and tribal partners, and private aquaculture in the areas of freshwater, estuarine and marine fish genetics, fish culture and fish health. Stakeholders, scientific review groups and numerous FWS internal documents affirm the importance of these facilities. However, this emphasis is not reflected by the FWS in its funding or in its establishment of priorities. Fish health centers and fish technology centers presently lack the focus and cohesiveness that provide integrated conceptual foundations for the array of scientific endeavors these facilities conduct or could conduct. Failure to fund adequately the national brood-stock program compromises its ability to ensure product quality and integrity by assisting states and tribes to obtain viable, genetically appropriate and disease-free eggs. Adequate funding and other incentives also should be put in place to allow the fish technology and fish health centers to work more closely with universities that conduct similar activities.

8 FWS must maintain and enhance training for hatchery managers and other hatchery personnel to ensure that only the best science is used and that new science is transferred as quickly as possible to all units.

To help achieve this goal, training curricula should be enhanced at the FWS National Conservation Training Center to ensure that technical and scientific skills are improved and knowledge of proper facility and personnel management throughout the NFHS is continually updated and enhanced.

MITIGATION

9 Legislation is necessary to clarify various existing legislative mandates and FWS policies regarding mitigation. New legislation must articulate clearly the role of the NFHS in mitigating for federal water and other development projects and how these mitigation activities are to be funded. Costs for the entire range of activities associated with hatchery production and stocking for mitigation must be fully reimbursed by the party or parties responsible for the development project. However, until this legislation is enacted, the FWS must continue to fund the current mitigation responsibilities of the NFHS.

Congress has given FWS multiple legislative mandates, and the FWS has implemented conflicting policies regarding priorities for national fish hatcheries. One result is that national fish hatcheries that are required to mitigate for federally sponsored development projects also have been simultaneously charged by the FWS to engage in threatened and endangered species recovery. The FWS has a series of mitigation responsibilities that are poorly defined, lack funding mechanisms, and often direct a national fish hatchery to produce mitigation fish that may compete with native fish. New legislation must provide direction to specific hatcheries to explain why the mitigation activity is taking place, what fish are to be produced, for whom, how the production is to be incorporated into appropriate regional fishery management planning, and how the mitigation activity is to be funded.

In FY 1999, production from 38 national fish hatcheries (nearly 50 percent of the NFHS) totally or partially provided fish to mitigate for federally funded development projects. Of these, 13 provide fish for mitigation specifically identified in an act authorizing a dam (statutory mitigation), and 25 provide fish for mitigation not specifically identified in dam authorizations (de-facto mitigation). Costs are recovered or reimbursed, in whole or in part, for about one-third of these hatcheries, as defined by legislative directives or memoranda of agreement (Attachment 7). Remaining costs are paid directly from FWS Fisheries Program appropriations. However, because of funding shortfalls, hatcheries funded through regular appropriations are augmented by a variety of reciprocal arrangements with the states.

Six mitigation hatcheries in the Southeast provide an example of funding needs, having annual operations and maintenance costs of about $2.3 million. FWS estimates that $4.5 million annually is necessary to fully recover costs from project beneficiaries in the Southeast, not including a $5.8 million maintenance backlog. Information from the FWS' Southeast Region, based in part on the American Sportfishing Association's publication "The Economic Importance of Sport Fishing," indicates an annual economic benefit of more than $400 million from those six hatcheries.

The steering committee considered other options for meeting federal fishery mitigation responsibilities, including state or tribal assumption of fish production with full reimbursement. However, the steering committee could not recommend this alternative due to the complexities of federal law and state and tribal authorities as well as many other political, social and administrative barriers and variables. Nevertheless, if situations arose in which certain states or tribes were willing to assume these responsibilities on a reimbursable basis, such production programs would be required to adhere to the same principles of science and accountability governing national fish hatcheries. Furthermore, responsibility for these production programs would need to be mutually agreed to by the state or tribe, the FWS and the federal development sponsor. Such an arrangement would need to be described in a cooperative agreement subject to public review and comment.

10 Until legislation is enacted to require reimbursement, current funding for NFHS mitigation operations must be maintained and must not be redirected for any other purpose.

Currently, by internal FWS practice, the costs of rearing threatened or endangered species are borne by the NFHS budget. The result is that the FWS is attempting to meet the critical need for hatchery involvement in threatened and endangered species recovery by redirecting already-limited funds from other hatchery programs, such as mitigation. The spiral of decreasing FWS budgets for hatchery operations further compounds the strain on funding for mitigation operations, although mitigation is a primary and often statutory mandate for many national fish hatcheries. This situation is exacerbated further when state and tribal cooperators are increasingly asked or required by FWS to purchase fish food, distribute fish and offset other production costs, often without prior consultation.

"The importance of this focused report cannot be overlooked. We must initiate a long-term plan to enhance and protect our National Fish Hatchery System."

–CHARLES HARTER III, DIRECTOR, COASTAL CONSERVATION ASSOCIATION

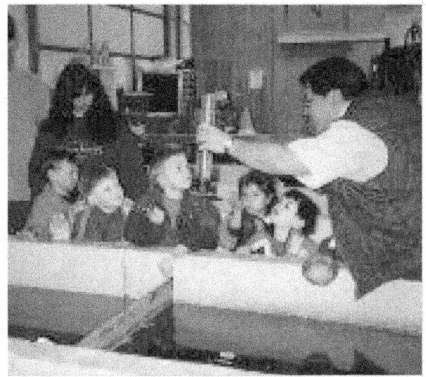

RECREATION AND OTHER COOPERATIVE PROGRAMS

11 Legislation must be enacted to provide the FWS with specific mandates that clarify the role of the NFHS in supporting and enhancing recreational fishing, in the context of the June 1995 Executive Order #12962 for Recreational Fisheries.

The steering committee agrees that the nation's fisheries are best served by using a holistic approach to fisheries management that includes restoring habitat and rebuilding fish populations. Current priorities in the FWS' Fisheries Program and the NFHS support this by focusing on restoration and recovery. However, the FWS retains certain responsibilities for providing recreational fishing opportunities in the United States.

Some of these responsibilities are legislatively or administratively mandated by statutes and executive orders, such as the Fish and Wildlife Act of 1956, Executive Order #12962, the National Wildlife Refuge System Improvement Act of 1997, tribal treaties, and other authorities, including the Sikes Act for support of recreational fishing on military and other federal lands. However, FWS presently fails to acknowledge recreational fishing as one of the priorities of the NFHS, and the national fish hatcheries' role in recreational fishing remains ambiguous. Although the FWS believes it provides recreational fishing opportunities as a result of its activities supporting mitigation, native fish restoration, and threatened and endangered species recovery, in the absence of clear policy guidance, decisions either to expand or reduce hatchery support for recreational fisheries have been arbitrary and politicized.

12 FWS should recover 100 percent of costs for production, stocking and any evaluation when providing fish to support purely recreational fishing programs (e.g. not as part of mitigation or restoration). Exceptions include meeting tribal trust responsibilities, stocking on national wildlife refuges, and providing fish for small, cooperative community service projects with education and outreach benefits, such as National Fishing Week events and scouting jamborees.

States and tribes have the predominant role in managing recreational fisheries within state and tribal boundaries. The Sikes Act requires FWS participation in fish and wildlife management planning on military lands, to include fish stocking, which occurs as a reimbursable activity. Although there is also an opportunity for national fish hatcheries to help support recreational fishing as defined above, it is not a federal responsibility. Therefore, the steering committee believes that these national fish hatchery expenses should be reimbursed.

13 Cooperative arrangements and exchanges between the FWS and states or tribes should continue as long as they are properly coordinated and planned. When fish are requested either by or from the FWS, the need must be defined in objectives in fishery management plans (Recommendation #1). Memoranda of agreement or other cooperative agreements between the FWS and its partners must define the general conditions for each exchange.

There are numerous existing exchange arrangements. Some are written into memoranda of understanding, some are contract cost agreements, and some are secured only by handshakes. All are considered partnerships and most represent good business practices and cooperation among partners. As indicated in the FWS' August 2000 Hatchery System Alignment report, many of these conservation exchanges and reimbursed activities are critical to the success of the FWS' partnerships with states, tribes, conservation organizations and universities. Other such exchanges also support the wise conservation of aquatic resources and ecosystems.

Cooperative exchanges also are often a cost-effective way of doing business. In managing fisheries resources to meet a variety of goals, sharing staff, equipment and hatchery-produced fish benefits the resource and resource users. Cooperative partnerships provide fisheries benefits such as exchanges of services, fish eggs, brood stock, fish health services, field work or fish transportation. However, when these exchanges are informal, random and uncoordinated, they can compromise sound business management and fiscal accountability. In some cases, there are no specific guidelines or sideboards defining this practice either at the regional or national level of the FWS. In a few cases, these arrangements have confused partners about the legitimate roles and responsibilities of the NFHS. These activities must be integrated into operational work plans (Recommendation #2) and reported in the system's annual performance report. The steering committee is optimistic that FWS work group products will help establish procedures to better manage these conservation partnerships.

> "I am deeply proud of the perseverance and vision the Council's hatchery project steering committee demonstrated throughout the entire process. Steering committee members and their employers donated many days of diligent work to cultivate the remarkable consensus achieved by the group. These experienced and committed fisheries leaders embraced the objective of instigating meaningful change for the National Fish Hatchery System."
>
> —HELEN SEVIER, CHAIR, SPORT FISHING AND BOATING PARTNERSHIP COUNCIL, BASS ANGLERS SPORTSMAN SOCIETY CHIEF EXECUTIVE OFFICER

THREATENED AND ENDANGERED SPECIES RECOVERY

14 The FWS must review threatened and endangered species recovery plan activities calling for the use of national fish hatcheries to assess the appropriateness of using a national fish hatchery for refugia or for using hatchery production for recovery and to determine the costs of doing so.

The steering committee recognizes threatened and endangered species recovery as an important and appropriate use of NFHS facilities. However, the FWS role in providing refugia and/or culturing threatened or endangered aquatic species in national fish hatcheries must be better defined and managed. Factors to be routinely considered must include the appropriateness and genetic implications of using culture as a recovery tool, the condition and capability of the habitat in sustaining recovery, the physical capabilities of a specific hatchery's facilities, and the scientific and technical capabilities of the hatchery's staff.

15 Fish production is no different from any other activity defined and funded as threatened and endangered species recovery. Therefore, endangered aquatic species recovery and refugia activities on national fish hatcheries must be funded by the FWS Endangered Species Program appropriation, consistent with other threatened and endangered species recovery activities conducted by the FWS.

The FWS, with assistance from state agencies, tribes and the recreational fishing and boating community, must seek appropriations to support hatchery-related activities for the conservation of threatened and endangered species in a way that does not divert dollars from other appropriate NFHS activities. The steering committee understands the need for the FWS to have funding discretion; however, it should not occur in a way that compromises other legislatively mandated activities of the NFHS.

16 The FWS, in consultation with recovery cooperators, must determine if state, tribal or private expertise can more effectively and economically provide necessary refugia or captive propagation for threatened or endangered species.

Culture of threatened and endangered species for recovery should not be confined to national fish hatcheries when other scientifically and technically capable facilities are available to meet production and recovery objectives with greater cost effectiveness. Although the FWS has a lead federal role in threatened and endangered species recovery, it does not automatically follow that the NFHS must have the only role in culture and refugia for these species.

NATIVE SPECIES RESTORATION

17 The NFHS must continue its role in restoration of interjurisdictional native fish species regardless of the availability of partnering funds. When national fish hatcheries cooperate in restoration of native species that are non-interjurisdictional but are of national significance, they must do the work under a cooperative agreement with the state or tribe.

There is an important role for the NFHS in restoration of native game and nongame fish in their aquatic habitats, and restoration should become an increasingly higher priority for the NFHS. However, restoration plans also must address physical, chemical, biological and harvest factors that impact species or communities. Artificial propagation and distribution is only one possible strategy in restoration planning. National fish hatchery programs should support watershed-based management, and these programs should be fully coordinated with state, tribal and other restoration efforts. The most cost-effective and ecologically and biologically effective approach to restoring imperiled species is to begin work before they become listed as threatened or endangered. The need to proactively manage and restore aquatic communities will only intensify as human populations continue to consume limited land and water resources.

FWS traditionally has focused its federal responsibility in cooperative restoration programs in interjurisdictional waters. Through its Fisheries Management Assistance Program and the NFHS, the FWS has made important contributions to restoring native fish species and aquatic communities. For non-interjurisdictional species restoration, national fish hatcheries should work cooperatively, at the request of states, tribes or other partners. In these cases, the lead agency should be the host state or tribe, not the FWS.

18 The NFHS should produce and stock fish to restore fisheries on national wildlife refuges, as outlined in restoration plans endorsed by regional management councils and/or interstate commissions, and to meet tribal trust or other obligations, regardless of the availability of partnership funds.

19 NFHS production should be reimbursed fully if it is directed at restoring a species within a single jurisdiction (non-interjurisdictional), that is not of national significance (i.e. not a potential candidate species or species of special concern), or does not fulfill a restoration plan endorsed by multiple state or tribal entities or commissions. Costs should include all aspects of fish production, stocking, and post-stocking evaluation and monitoring.

20 The FWS, in conjunction with states, tribes, interstate commissions, the National Marine Fisheries Service, and other partners, should develop the NFHS' potential role in the restoration and management of inter-jurisdictional estuarine and marine fisheries.

FWS currently has the authority to cooperate and participate in coastal estuarine and marine fisheries management activities. There is an opportunity for exploring potential uses of the NFHS in an expanding role in coastal and marine fisheries management. FWS should consult its partners, as opportunities and needs for restoration production in coastal and marine environments escalate, to help prioritize production from national fish hatcheries. In cases where more definition has been needed to engage the NFHS, Congress has provided clear authority for the FWS in nationally significant species restoration programs, such as the Emergency Striped Bass Act. This program has worked well, and it is likely that similar efforts will be needed in the future.

SUMMARY

The steering committee's recommendations chart a significant new course for the NFHS. This new course recognizes the system's vital roles in fulfilling mitigation obligations; restoring and maintaining native fisheries; giving priority to recreational fisheries; strengthening cooperation with states, tribes and partners; and improving accountability with Congress, NFHS stakeholders and the general public.

A repeated theme throughout the report is the essential requirement to produce and use cultured products from the NFHS in a way that uses the best possible science-based management principles and practices. The recommendations emphasize the crucial role the fish technology centers, fish health centers, and the national brood-stock programs play. The steering committee believes these services are vital to improving the science of fish culture and fisheries management programs that use cultured products and encourages the FWS to increase attention and funding for these programs.

Report recommendations acknowledge the NFHS' role in mitigation but ask for legislative clarification of that responsibility, as well as authority to assure full cost recovery for mitigation-related expenses from the parties responsible for development projects.

Federally funded implementation of threatened and endangered species recovery plans is noted as an appropriate and important use of the NFHS. It is recommended that in the future the important role the system plays in the recovery of threatened and endangered aquatic species be funded from threatened and endangered species program appropriations.

The long-term stability of the NFHS will be further solidified by implementing the steering committee's recommendations that acknowledge the significant role the system has and should have in restoration of native fisheries. It is also recommended that Congress clarify the role the NFHS should play in supporting recreational fishing objectives.

With regard to tribal trust responsibilities, the steering committee recommends that the FWS work closely with affected tribes to ensure that the responsibilities of the NFHS, with regard to tribal trust and treaty agreements, is clarified and properly implemented.

Finally, the steering committee believes that outreach and accountability are critical to the success and future of the NFHS. The FWS must manage the system in a way that promotes cooperation and communication with stakeholders and partners in reporting on the system's needs and achievements and in identifying the priorities, goals and objectives for the system.

"This report is extremely important to the states. However, of even greater importance is Congress' willingness to support the report's recommendations legislatively and give clear direction to the Fish and Wildlife Service regarding the roles, responsibilities and operation of the National Fish Hatchery System."

–GARY MYERS, EXECUTIVE DIRECTOR, TENNESSEE WILDLIFE RESOURCES AGENCY REPRESENTATIVE, INTERNATIONAL ASSOCIATION OF FISH AND WILDLIFE AGENCIES

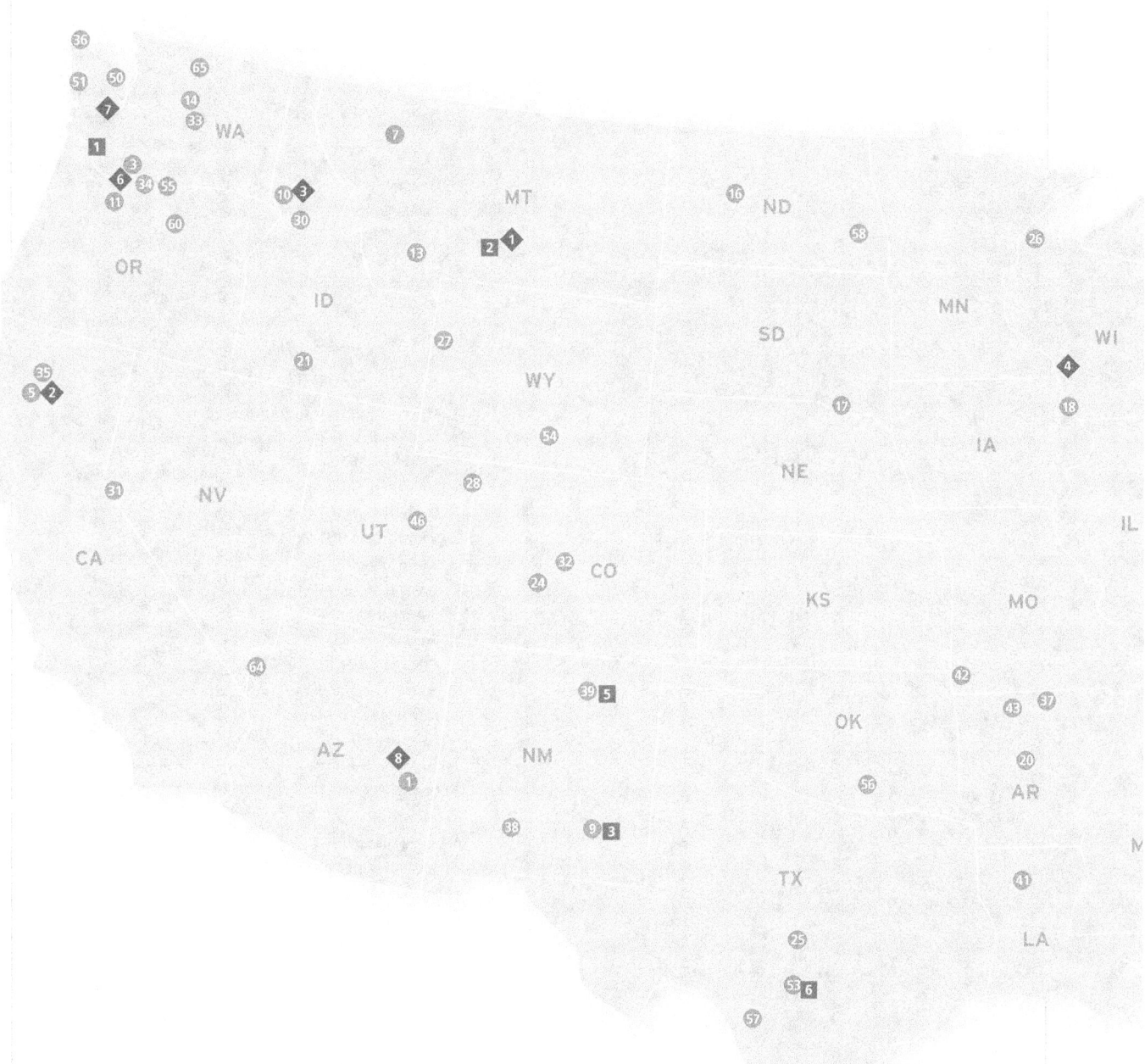

SPORT FISHING AND BOATING PARTNERSHIP COUNCIL

NATIONAL FISH HATCHERY SYSTEM MAP

● NATIONAL FISH HATCHERIES

1　Alchesay-Williams Creek NFH, AZ
2　Allegheny NFH, PA
3　Carson NFH, WA
4　Chattahoochee Forest NFH, GA
5　Coleman NFH, CA
6　Craig Brook NFH, ME
7　Creston NFH, MT
8　Dale Hollow NFH, TN
9　Dexter NFH, NM
10　Dworshak NFH, ID
11　Eagle Creek NFH, OR
12　Edenton NFH, NC
13　Ennis NFH, MT
14　Entiat NFH, WA
15　Erwin NFH, TN
16　Garrison Dam NFH, ND
17　Gavins Point NFH, SD
18　Genoa NFH, WI
19　Green Lake NFH, ME
20　Greers Ferry NFH, AR
21　Hagerman NFH, ID
22　Harrison Lake NFH, VA
23　Hiawatha Forest NFH, MI
24　Hotchkiss NFH, CO
25　Inks Dam NFH, TX
26　Iron River NFH, WI
27　Jackson NFH, WY
28　Jones Hole NFH, UT
29　Jordan River NFH, MI
30　Kooskia NFH, ID
31　Lahontan NFH, NV
32　Leadville NFH, CO
33　Leavenworth NFH, WA
34　Little White Salmon NFH, WA
35　Livingston Stone NFH, CA
36　Makah NFH, WA
37　Mammoth Spring NFH, AR
38　Mescalero NFH, NM
39　Mora NFH, NM
40　Nashua NFH, NH
41　Natchitoches NFH, LA
42　Neosho NFH, MO

43　Norfork NFH, AR
44　North Attleboro NFH, MA
45　Orangeburg NFH, SC
46　Ouray NFH, UT
47　Pendills Creek NFH, MI
48　Pittsford NFH, VT
49　Private John Allen NFH, MS
50　Quilcene NFH, WA
51　Quinault NFH, WA
52　Richard Cronin NSS, MA
53　San Marcos NFH, TX
54　Saratoga NFH, WY
55　Spring Creek NFH, WA
56　Tishomingo NFH, OK
57　Uvalde NFH, TX
58　Valley City NFH, ND
59　Warm Springs NFH, GA
60　Warm Springs NFH, OR
61　Welaka NFH, FL
62　White River NFH, VT
63　White Sulphur Springs NFH, WV
64　Willow Beach NFH, AZ
65　Winthrop NFH, WA
66　Wolf Creek NFH, KY

■ FISH TECHNOLOGY CENTERS

1　Abernathy FTC, WA
2　Bozeman FTC, MT
3　Dexter FTC, NM
4　Lamar FTC, PA
5　Mora FTC, NM
6　San Marcos FTC, TX
7　Warm Springs FTC, GA

◆ FISH HEALTH CENTERS

1　Bozeman FHC, MT
2　California-Nevada FHC, CA
3　Idaho FHC, ID
4　La Crosse FHC, WI
5　Lamar FTC, PA
6　Lower Columbia River FHC, WA
7　Olympia FHC, WA
8　Pinetop FHC, AZ
9　Warm Springs FHC, GA

U.S. House of Representatives
Committee on Resources
Washington, DC 20515

March 18, 1999

The Honorable David M. Walker
Comptroller General
United States General Accounting Office
441 G Street, Northwest
Washington, DC 20548

Dear Mr. Walker:

This is a formal request for the General Accounting Office to produce a report which will serve as a baseline for evaluating whether the National Fish Hatchery System is meeting the Fish and Wildlife Service's present objectives. My hope and intention is that the results of this report may lead Congress to work closely with the Fish and Wildlife Service and the Fisheries Program to consider any appropriate changes in existing law to refine and clarify their legal mandates.

My intention in requesting this review is to provide a baseline assessment of current Fisheries activities from which to work proactively with the Fish and Wildlife Service and other stakeholders to plan out the short and long term goals of the Fisheries Program and the National Fish Hatchery System. Fish culture and stocking may be legitimate tools for fisheries managers when used responsibly and with the support of solid scientific evaluation of their effectiveness.

However, stocking is also a very different type of management tool than regulation, enforcement, or habitat management and should neither replace nor supercede these other important activities. I also believe that the Service is obligated not to use enhancement as a permanent alternative to habitat protection or restoration, although I do understand that there are many situations in which supplementation programs are justly used to fulfill federal obligations in mitigating the impacts of federal projects. In general, I support the work that the Service and the Fisheries Program have done in restoring aquatic species and ecosystems, and make this request only with the intention of improving on their performance and effectiveness in their many difficult tasks.

With this in mind, I would appreciate your taking into consideration the following requests for information:

1. To better permit an understanding of trends in current activities within the National Fish Hatchery System, please provide me with a simple evaluation of this division's spending trends related to hatcheries and mitigation -- and compared to the rest of the Fisheries Program -- over the last five to 10 years. To the extent practicable, please elaborate on the degree to which the Service believes that inadequate funding was or may have been a factor in failing to reach the objectives of fisheries program and management activities.

2. In order to carefully evaluate the Service's current activities, please delineate, using either fish eggs or pounds of fish, production by the NFHS in 1998 for each of the categories below. To the extent practicable, I would also like to know the final destination of this production, in other words whether it was delivered to federal waters, state waters, tribal waters, or private waters.

- Restoration and recovery of threatened and endangered species mandated by the Endangered Species Act
- Supplementation or enhancement of native species
- Enhancement of non-native species
- Mandated mitigation, including court orders, for both native and non-native species and the ecosystems upon which they depend
- Recreational activities such as put and take or put and grow
- Research and development activities
- Reimbursed activities paid for by states, tribes, or other entities

The Fish and Wildlife Service has carefully defined terms used in the list above in an effort to avoid double-counting when relevant (i.e. separates restoration and supplementation so that production for each do not overlap). The information is attached.

3. An evaluation of the appropriate laws which authorize and direct the activities of the Fisheries Program and National Fish Hatchery System, and the process through which the Service ensures that NFHS activities are consistent with these and other applicable laws such as the Endangered Species Act and the National Environmental Protection Act. To the extent practicable, this evaluation should include an analysis of the extent to which the GAO believes that the actions and results of the Fisheries Program and National Fish Hatchery System are consistent with the law.

I would also like to receive an estimate of what percentage of each of the categories in request 2 includes projects or activities where the ultimate goal is *not* attaining self-sustaining populations or natural reproduction.

5. Finally, I would like an analysis of the process through which the Fisheries Program determines which approach, or approaches, are appropriate to use in managing aquatic resources. This would presumably include evaluating how hatchery or program managers define the objectives of their enhancement programs and determine how success of a program's objectives will be determined. For example, if the objective of an enhancement program is restoration, but no specific criteria are established or monitored to determine when restoration is achieved, there can be no way of knowing when restoration has succeeded and stocking should be discontinued. In such cases, stocking may occur indefinitely and thus be considered a "put and take" activity.

While I have real concerns that funding needs for operations such as threatened and endangered species recovery are not being met, I also recognize that the overall funding for operational and maintenance needs throughout the Fisheries Program is likely to be inadequate. Our desire is to help the fisheries program acquire the resources they need to successfully reach their objectives, while simultaneously ensuring that these objectives are consistent with sound natural resource management principals.

I greatly appreciate your assistance in this matter, and I and my staff look forward to working out any further details or problems concerning this request with you in the near future.

Sincerely,

GEORGE MILLER
Senior Democratic Member

Congress of the United States
Washington, DC 20515

May 26, 1999

Ms. Jamie R. Clark, Director
U.S. Fish and Wildlife Service
Mail Stop 3012
1849 C Street, NW
Washington, D.C. 20240

Dear Ms. Clark:

At a time when we continue to make significant strides in boosting the responsible stewardship of America's fish and wildlife resources with a broad array of conservation partners, we are writing to ask for your support of a broad and balanced review of the National Fish Hatchery System that would make some determinations and recommendations about its proper role and overall mission in the conservation of America's fishery resources.

What would become the nation's first fish hatchery was created in 1872 with the establishment of a salmon egg collecting station on the McCloud River in California. In the 127 years since then, more than 280 hatcheries have been established to ensure the restoration of self-sustaining fish populations and the replacement of depleted or lost fisheries resources that are a result of federal development projects. Today, the U.S. Fish and Wildlife Service manages 66 fish hatcheries, which play an integral role in the agency's statutory obligations regarding the restoration, recovery, and mitigation of fishery resources.

We understand that there is a wide and diverse field of opinion among many different stake-holders when it comes to the proper role, scope, and mission, of the National Fish Hatchery System. We are aware that the Service is nearing completion of its Alignment, Appropriateness, and Adequacy Evaluation (the 3 A's), and that U.S. Rep. George Miller of California has asked the General Accounting Office to review the role and scope of the hatchery system. We believe that those are positive, important, and needed steps; if we are to set a viable, long-term course for the future of the hatchery system. We are also aware of your intention outlined in a May 25th Service-wide memorandum to refocus the future direction of the hatchery system. We are convinced as well that there should be one additional piece to this process.

With all of that in mind, we are recommending that an open, inclusive, and participatory dialogue be launched that builds on the "3 A's" evaluation and incorporates the results of the GAO review with the ultimate goal being to determine just what the future-role of our fish hatchery system should be given the restoration, recovery, and mitigation needs it is not only currently addressing, but will be expected to meet well into the 21st Century.

We think it would benefit all stake-holders to convene a diverse committee that includes a broad spectrum of views regarding the hatchery system's future role from state fish and wildlife agencies and fisheries experts within the Service to fisheries conservation and angling organizations like Trout Unlimited, B.A.S.S., the American Sportfishing Association, the Izaak Walton League of America, and the American Fisheries Society. We suspect that this process will not always be simple and painless. Nevertheless, it is one that should be undertaken with the kind of inclusiveness that led to the enactment of the National Wildlife Refuge System Improvement Act of 1997. Once we are armed with the best scientific information, our fisheries managers will be able to chart a clear course with a well-defined mission for America's hatchery system that will allow it to meet its restoration, recovery, and mitigation obligations even better.

So in that spirit, we are soliciting your support in the facilitation of a process aimed at developing a clear vision and mission for the future role of the National Fish Hatchery System. It is our view that the successful partnerships we have relied upon to achieve important fisheries conservation achievements to date, will be needed to assure the fisheries conservation goals of the future.

Thank you for your important advocacy on behalf of our natural resources, and we look forward to hearing from you soon.

Sincerely,

cc: Cathleen Short, Assistant Director for Fisheries

United States Department of the Interior

FISH AND WILDLIFE SERVICE

Washington, D.C. 20240

In Reply Refer To:
FWS/AEA

Ms. Helen Sevier   AUG 17 1999
Chairman and CEO
B.A.S.S., Incorporated
5845 Carmichael Road
Montgomery, Alabama 36117

Dear Ms. Sevier:

The Fish and Wildlife Service commends you and the Sport Fishing and Boating
Partnership Council on the development of the *Strategic Plan for the National Outreach
and Communications Program* and for the Council's past work under the President's
Executive Order 12962. Since its inception in 1993, the Council has become a vital force
to represent anglers' and boaters' concerns for aquatic resource conservation.

As evidenced by its work under the Executive Order and through the exhaustive efforts
undertaken to develop the Strategic Plan, the Council has proven its ability to engage
stakeholders successfully in a process to develop important consensus-based
recommendations about a variety of recreational fishing, boating and aquatic resource
conservation issues.

The Service is currently developing a strategic plan for the National Fish Hatchery System
that will prepare the system to meet its responsibilities more effectively in the coming
years. We desire to be inclusive with this effort and ask that you once again undertake to
build consensus among natural resource stakeholders to provide recommendations that will
assist in the development of the strategic plan. We hope that the Council's ability to
coalesce stakeholders to develop visionary approaches to aquatic resource conservation
challenges will result in recommendations that frame the National Fish Hatchery System's
role in fulfilling not only the Service's aquatic resource conservation obligations, but the
system's role in fisheries and aquatic resources conservation in general.

Looking ahead, we would hope the Council's full report containing recommendations to
the Service and the Secretary could be completed by August of 2000, with an interim report

available by March 1, 2000. We request that this consensus-building process be an open, inclusive dialogue that incorporates recent internal and external reviews and evaluations of the hatchery system. We leave it up to you to develop the process that will ultimately result in these recommendations. In addition, we ask that the Council take full advantage of the coordination and integration opportunities provided by the Service work groups recently formed to assemble data and other information about the National Fish Hatchery System.

Please contact us if you wish to discuss this request in more detail. The Service will assist you as the Council moves forward on this issue. We look forward to supporting the Council as it undertakes this important work.

Sincerely,

DIRECTOR

Sport Fishing and Boating Partnership Council

Sept. 2, 1999

Dr. John G. Rogers
Acting Director
U.S. Fish and Wildlife Service
1849 C St., N.W., MS 3012
Washington, D.C. 20240

Dear John,

Thank you very much for your August 17 letter.

The Sport Fishing and Boating Partnership Council stands ready, as requested in your letter, to facilitate an open, inclusive national process to provide recommendations regarding the future of the National Fish Hatchery System. To this process, the Council will bring its financial, staff and volunteer resources, as well as its demonstrated ability to conductsuccessful national, facilitated discussions and to offer recommendations about issues related to aquatic resource conservation policy.

The Council recognizes that this process is necessary to address the long-term needs and purposes of the National Fish Hatchery System. The Council believes that creating a new, comprehensive, consensus-based blueprint for the hatchery system and developing a method to move the system from its current state toward a new strategic plan will be at the heart of this process. This process will build on previous years' research, relevant Service and other documents, recommendations and input from stakeholders, the "three As" evaluation and the General Accounting Office review. In addition, the Council is looking forward to interacting frequently with the Service's Fisheries Program's work groups tasked with assembling data and other information about the National Fish Hatchery System.

The Council is now developing a work plan to carry out this task in a way that will conform to your request for a full report and final recommendations to the Secretary of the Interior by August 2000, with an interim report available by March 1, 2000. Once it is completed, the work plan will be shared with you and members of your staff.

The Council is eager to begin work on this important topic and will provide you with regular updates as we embark on this project.

Sincerely,

Helen Sevier

Helen Sevier
Chair, SFBPC

Summary of Previous Reports and Recommendations
Regarding the National Fish Hatchery System

A myriad of studies, reports and recommendations from outside groups and from Fish and Wildlife Service (FWS) appointed committees and task forces have been undertaken in an attempt to help guide the FWS and the National Fish Hatchery System. The most prominent of those reports are discussed here, briefly. A comprehensive compilation of recommendations from the principal reports review by the steering committee follows this discussion.

Calhoun Report: In January 1974, a task force of five individuals was formed representing the American Fisheries Society, the International Association of Fish and Wildlife Agencies, state fish and wildlife agencies, and the Sport Fishing Institute. Fisheries consultant Alex Calhoun chaired the task force. The group was asked to "...examine the national program for fish culture and directly related activities...to review state and federal roles and responsibilities and to recommend any changes needed to achieve maximum efficiency through a coordinated national program whose state and federal components supplement each other fully while avoiding duplication of effort."

The report concluded that longstanding policy assigning top priority for distribution of National Fish Hatchery System fish to waters under federal jurisdiction was poorly implemented and needed to be "...reviewed and revised to provide more substantial and meaningful program goals...." The report made 31 recommendations to better define federal/state roles.

Responsibilities and Roles: In 1985, in the face of declining budgets, the FWS reviewed its Fishery Resources Program, with a goal of assuring its responsibilities and role were properly "scoped and focused." The result was identification of responsibilities that would "henceforth be the focus of the Service's reoriented Fishery Resources Program":

- Facilitate restoration of depleted, nationally significant fishery resources.

- Seek mitigation for fishery resource impairment due to federal water-related development.

- Assist with management of fishery resources of federal (primarily FWS) and tribal lands.

- Maintain federal leadership in scientific management of national fishery resources.

These standards continue to guide the FWS Fisheries Program. Although the document contained little discussion of the role of national fish hatcheries, it recognized their role in fish health and technology development as part of FWS leadership in scientifically based management.

Action Plan for Fishery Resources and Aquatic Ecosystems: In May 1994, the FWS once again examined its Fisheries Program to redirect activities toward an "ecosystem approach" based on healthy aquatic habitats. The action plan delineated program elements for the National Fish Hatchery System, some of which are followed today: "…an innovative propagation program that supports native species restoration; endangered species recovery; Federal mitigation responsibilities; subsistence, commercial, and recreational fishing; monitoring and assessment programs; and National Wildlife Refuge and Tribal needs." One of the highest priorities was "maintaining healthy wild populations through genetic diversity, harvest management, habitat improvements, and judicious use of hatchery stocks."

Components 4 and 5 in the Fishery Management Support section of the action plan provided priorities for the National Fish Hatchery System. What is implicit in these was affirmation that national fish hatcheries should support fishery and aquatic resource management. Only species, stocks, strains, races and numbers of fish deemed compatible with and identified in ecosystem management plans would be produced.

National Fish and Wildlife Foundation Report: That same year, the FWS director also asked the National Fish and Wildlife Foundation to convene a review panel to do an "outside objective evaluation" of the National Fish Hatchery System and make recommendations for its future role in ecosystem management. The report concluded that "…it is clear the national fish hatchery program needs a new edict. That edict must recognize the need for fundamental redirection of programs, personnel, and facilities toward supporting ecosystem management whether it relates to restoring depleted populations of anadromous fishes or the recovery of threatened and endangered species." This report focused on outside reactions as to what national fish hatcheries were doing and illustrated that there is a lack of understanding of how national fish hatcheries fit into a fishery management program.

The foundation's report concluded that despite the existence of program management documents, vision statements, policy statements and generic management plans, a "…well-defined national fisheries program with definite goals, objectives, implementation and evaluation strategies does not appear to exist." This statement accurately characterizes the FWS program, of which national fish hatcheries are only the production component.

Compilation of Recommendations and Conclusions from Previous Reports Regarding the National Fish Hatchery System

Documents reviewed to compile this comparison included:

1974 Report of National Task Force for Public Fish Hatchery Policy (Calhoun)

1985 FWS Statement of Responsibilities and Role (R&R)

1991 Department of Interior Inspector General Audit on Recovery of Mitigation Costs for Bureau of Reclamation Projects (IG)

1994 Action Plan for Fishery Resources and Aquatic Ecosystems (AP)

1994 Report of the National Fish Hatchery Review Panel (NFWF)

1996-97 Recommendations from FWS Stakeholders Meetings (SM)

1999 General Accounting Office Report on Distribution of Fish and Fish Eggs Needs (GAO)

The compilation is arranged by category to facilitate use by steering committee work groups: Introduction; Scientific Leadership and Stocking Protocols; Mitigation and Recreation; Threatened, Endangered and Native Species; and Funding Considerations. Recommendations are duplicated where they may apply to more than one category. When they didn't seem to fit existing categories, they were put into the Introduction section. Recommendations are paraphrased.

INTRODUCTION (and miscellaneous):

· FWS and National Marine Fisheries Service (NMFS), in concert with states, define problems associated with inadequate intercommunications in the national program for fish culture and formulate solutions. (Calhoun)

· A position/policy statement should be made by the FWS declaring that the primary mission of hatcheries into the next century will be to provide fish for support of ecosystem management and habitat restoration. (NFWF)

· Hatcheries not needed to meet current or redirected program needs should be considered candidates for closure or transfer to states. (NFWF)

· Changes in FWS policies and provision of hatchery fish should be done with discussion and negotiations with affected states and other partners. Proposed changes should be time-phased to accommodate needs of states or tribes. (NFWF)

· Changes in policies regarding providing or using federally produced fish by states should be implemented only after states have been fully informed well in advance. Adequate lead time should be allowed for states to assume any new responsibilities. If the change involves transfer of a facility to a state, a negotiated phase-in should be part of the changeover from full federal support through shared cost to full state takeover. (NFWF)

· Lead federal responsibility for assisting private aquaculture should be in U.S. Department of Agriculture (USDA). (NFWF)

· A new public outreach and education approach is needed to emphasize the role of federal hatcheries as vital support to resource managers in aquatic ecosystem stewardship, not just as fish-raising and stocking stations. (NFWF)

· Stakeholders strongly suggest others taking the lead in providing general aquatic education. (SM)

· The FWS will develop a process to ensure timely and effective stakeholder input into FWS decisions on a continuing basis. (SM)

- Establish partnerships with the private aquaculture community to ensure industry development that is economically viable and compatible with protection of native and wild fish populations. (AP)

- Establish environmental awareness and outreach programs to develop an informed and involved citizenry that supports aquatic ecosystem conservation and fishery stewardship. (AP)

- Legislative authorities for fishery responsibilities are vague. Stakeholders offered to work with the FWS to establish clear authorities and pursue legislation where appropriate. The FWS said it was receptive to pursuing clarifying legislative authority and would support the effort of others to develop and submit legislation to establish specific authorities for fishery activities, particularly those not covered by the Fish and Wildlife Coordination Act. (SM)

- Deciding what course of action to take in the face of declining operations and maintenance appropriations requires, among other things, a clear understanding of the role and responsibilities of federal hatcheries. However, information on how federal hatcheries have been supporting the FWS' programs through the distribution of fish and fish eggs has not been reliable and does not provide a clear picture of the unique role that federal hatcheries are supposed to fill. To provide the Congress with the information needed to evaluate the appropriate role of the National Fish Hatchery System, we recommend that the Secretary of the Interior direct the Director of the Fish and Wildlife Service to take steps to refine the classification system for fish and fish egg distribution and help ensure that hatchery managers appropriately classify all fish and fish egg distribution by its principal purpose. (GAO)

Scientific Leadership and Stocking Protocols

- Explore, in concert with states, various ways in which the federal level can assist in coordinating fish culture programs that interlock many states. (Calhoun)

- FWS and NMFS increase emphasis on research and development related to culture of Pacific salmon and steelhead; encourage and participate in state-federal review of existing and proposed projects in this field; encourage and participate in development of a state-federal system for jointly assigning priorities and responsibilities for research and development. (Calhoun)

- That the federal government, in concert with states, strengthen its role in research and development relating to fish culture; further, that the state and federal agencies concerned look to the advantages of geographical and problem coordination of their research and development efforts. (Calhoun)

- FWS review goals and operations of its developmental program for fish culture to determine whether it will function better under regional or central leadership. (Calhoun)

- FWS, with NMFS, assign a much higher priority to development of procedures for culturing larvae of striped bass and midrange species using artificial diets. (Calhoun)

- Each state or federal agency assume responsibility for routine disease control in its own hatchery system. (Calhoun)

- FWS, with NMFS and in concert with states and private sector, set up a problem-solving team of individuals knowledgeable about technical, social, and political aspects of national fish disease problems, directing this team to develop plans for an action program, including any corrective legislation that may be necessary to control the spread of the more serious diseases. (Calhoun)

- FWS, in concert with states, continue to develop and strengthen national system for disease appraisal and certification of salmonid eggs. (Calhoun)

- FWS continue important role of maintaining disease-free brood stocks and providing states with disease-free eggs to start their own brood stocks, but FWS not attempt to become a routine source of supply for disease-free eggs or fingerlings for production purposes. (Calhoun)

- States and FWS assume responsibility for training their respective employees; FWS continue to provide opportunities for nonfederal workers to participate in its training sessions related to fish culture and disease control. (Calhoun)

- Work more closely with other governmental agencies and private organizations to restore habitat of depleted native stocks, rather than rely on hatchery fish to compensate for habitat losses. (NFWF)

- Maintain and make available the full range of expertise required to protect and manage fishery resources, including that in fish culture and fishery resource management; maintain the well-established scientific institution it now represents, with core capability in all the disciplines required, to effectively contribute to protecting the productivity and maximizing the potential of fishery resources. (R&R)

- Maintain brood stocks representing all major species for use in special management situations, giving development of different strains or modification of genetic character major consideration. (R&R)

- Develop new concepts and improved technology in fishery resource management and fish propagation (stock assessment, allocation options, chemical/drug registration). (R&R)

- Provide leadership in technology of fish disease diagnosis and fish health practice, for application in cooperation with other entities to control spread of diseases, including certification of fish disease inspectors. (R&R)

- Develop policies to address introduction and control of exotic species, uniform practices in fish health, and standardization of fishery statistics. (R&R)

- Make technical assistance available to other natural resource agencies and organizations, transfer technical information through advanced training in fishery management and fish culture through the fisheries academy. (R&R)

- Stocking fish on federal lands should be consistent with an approved aquatic ecosystem management plan, precluding deleterious competitive and genetic effects of stocked fish on native species. Fish from wild populations should be used as brood stock to maintain genetic diversity. When species or stocks are brought into captivity, fish health personnel should be involved so vital data on disease status, habitat requirements, behavior and spawning habits will be available when needed. (NFWF)

- Develop a comprehensive fisheries program that defines the numbers and stocks of fish needed to support an ecosystem management concept and define how to better integrate hatchery products and fish hatchery expertise into the ecosystem management program. (NFWF)

- Integrate and implement the Action Plan for Fisheries and Aquatic Resources into the new ecosystem management concept immediately. (NFWF)

- Regional ecosystem management teams should evaluate each hatchery in a region and determine if the unit and its products are compatible with resource and ecosystem needs. Any unit that fails to meet these tests should be considered as potentially excess to the FWS. (NFWF)

- Evaluate hatcheries to determine if production could be consolidated to increase efficiency without loss in quality, no net loss in production needs, and no loss in genetic diversity of species, stocks, or strains. (NFWF)

- As part of reprogramming funds and divesting facilities, hatcheries not needed to meet specific program needs or to assist in prevention of further stock decline or to propagate threatened and endangered species should be evaluated for possible use as research sites for development of culture methods for nontraditional aquatic organisms, as study sites, or as centers for habitat evaluation and restoration. Realignment of facility uses should be tied to technology development center programs. (NFWF).

- Fisheries resources in the regional offices should determine the numbers, species, stocks, strains, races, etc., needed to support and achieve goals and objectives of ecosystem management in the regions. (NFWF)

- Using native populations for brood fish requires knowledge of the health status of the wild fish. Fish Disease Control Center personnel should be involved in health evaluations and selection of potential brood fish to ensure hatcheries produce fish free of introduced diseases and parasites. (NFWF)

- After-stocking evaluations should be conducted to evaluate how well hatchery-produced fish achieve program goals. (NFWF)

- Do not discontinue fish health services to nonfederal clients until state or private capabilities are in place. Once they are, fish health centers should decline to provide further assistance. (NFWF)

- Private aquaculture should be given greater access to disease-free stocks and strains maintained in the federal brood-stock registry and to other stocks in national fish hatcheries to help control spread of specific pathogens to native populations and ecosystems. (NFWF)

- Establish an interagency group with U.S. Department of Agriculture to ensure goals and activities of private aquaculture include consideration and prevention of potential impacts from accidental establishment of feral populations on native populations. (NFWF)

- Encourage and increase efforts to share federal hatchery expertise with others through publications in journals, newsletters, workshops, etc. Strategic outreach for dissemination of scientific and public education materials should be developed. (NFWF)

- Hatchery managers and employees must be kept informed as to their roles in the FWS' ecosystem approach. Hatcheries have the capability to reprogram and are ready to become an integral part of ecosystem management. (NFWF)

- Ensure that FWS' hatchery and management programs are based on approved management plans and are compatible with preservation of native and wild populations. (AP)

- Ensure production of hatchery fish and associated management are based on integrated principles of conservation genetics and ecology. (AP)

- Develop and implement monitoring, sampling, and reporting systems to evaluate effectiveness of (1) fishery restoration, mitigation and enhancement programs and (2) hatchery programs in achieving specific management objectives, especially in conserving wild stocks, maintaining the diversity of native fish communities, and contributing to stable, productive fisheries. (AP)

- Develop and implement a FWS conservation genetics policy to ensure that management and hatchery programs contribute to: (1) national fishery objectives, (2) fishery objectives for specific ecosystems, and (3) preservation of genetic diversity and integrity. (AP)

- Develop and use captive propagation techniques for fishes and other aquatic species listed as threatened, endangered, or candidate under the Endangered Species Act, when specifically prescribed in recovery plans. Other techniques that are in accordance with conservation genetic principles and in conjunction with habitat restoration may be approved by the FWS director. (AP)

- Support investigations in genetics, threatened and endangered fish, drug and chemical management, water and effluent management, wild and cultured fish interactions, hatchery product evaluation, and non-indigenous aquatic nuisance species management. (AP)

- Design and implement innovative fishery technology development activities to support conservation and restoration of aquatic ecosystems. (AP)

- Establish fish health programs and protocols to protect wild and hatchery populations from diseases. Develop technologies and procedures to minimize risk of pathogen transfer to avoid or minimize epizootic outbreaks. (AP)

- Develop predictive capabilities to determine the cumulative effects of habitat degradation and alteration on fishery resources and aquatic ecosystems. (AP)

- Develop assessment and predictive capabilities to determine methods of preventing introductions of and controlling or eliminating nonindigenous aquatic nuisance species as well as determining their effects on aquatic resources. (AP)

- Develop and implement protocols to ensure that fish, fish pathogens, and fish products from private aquaculture operations do not pose unacceptable risks to natural ecosystems. (AP)

- Provide fish culture information, fish containment techniques, results of fish health research, technical training, and technical assistance to private aquaculture consistent with FWS fishery stewardship objectives. (AP)

· Tribal leaders want the FWS to emphasize training in natural resource management to enable tribes to become self-sufficient in managing their own resources. (SM)

· Fish health support from the FWS is highly valued by states, private aquaculture, and others, with emphasis on wild fish in rivers and coastal areas and cultured fish. Because alternative sources for fish health inspections currently exist, the FWS does not see providing inspections to states and private aquaculture as a high-priority responsibility. However, the FWS will continue to provide diagnostic support and virology inspections as resources permit until alternate sources are available. (SM)

· Identify, in conjunction with stakeholders, future needs for technology, technical assistance, data management, and research for fishery resources and identify alternative ways of meeting those needs. (SM)

Mitigation and Recreation

· States assume full management and financial responsibility for stocking inland public fishing waters within their boundaries except for special situations that justify assistance from federal or local government or private utilities or other appropriate sources. (Calhoun)

· Public fishing waters on federal lands be treated like any other public waters for purposes of fishery management, and states assume full responsibility for stocking them, except for large federally developed reservoirs or situations where such action is precluded by statute; further, that responsibilities be shifted in a manner that does not abruptly burden any state financially. (Calhoun)

· States assume full responsibility for managing fisheries in federal reservoirs within their boundaries, but FWS assist with stocking programs as required to develop and maintain optimal recreational potential of such waters. However, in line with the heavy state responsibility, federal contribution should not exceed the state contribution. All cooperative stocking programs for federal reservoirs should be formalized by interagency agreements defining justification and the kinds and amounts of fish to be provided by the state and the FWS. (Calhoun)

· States be responsible for stocking public fishing waters on state boundaries, which should be treated like other public fishing waters. However, the FWS should stand ready to coordinate stocking programs involving a number of states, when asked. (Calhoun)

· States assume responsibility for providing fish for initial stocking of warmwater fishes on military reservations with restricted public access; further, the users assume financial responsibility for stocking such waters with trout and other fish that need to be planted repeatedly. (Calhoun)

· When national policy dictates that fish reared at public expense be stocked on tribal lands, federal hatcheries provide such fish in situations where the state desires them to do so, but only in accordance with a sound, predeveloped fishery management plan. (Calhoun)

· Existing federal stocking programs for tribal lands be evaluated from economic and fishery management standpoints. (Calhoun)

· Decisions concerning stocking responsibilities on national parks and monuments be made by federal and state agencies concerned with them on the basis of local circumstances. (Calhoun)

- FWS continue to implement decision to remove federal responsibility for stocking farm ponds, in a manner that does not abruptly burden any state financially. (Calhoun)

- FWS adopt a policy prohibiting stocking federal fish in private waters lacking public access. (Calhoun)

- FWS not provide fish for put-and-take programs, except in large federal reservoirs under heavy fishing pressure when the state cannot develop optimal recreational potential without assistance; FWS should not provide more than half the fish. (Calhoun)

- FWS not provide fish for put-and-take stocking in urban areas or for urban recreational programs. (Calhoun)

- Federal and state governments continue to share responsibility for culture of Pacific salmon and steelhead. (Calhoun)

- Federal and state governments continue to share responsibility for producing Atlantic salmon smolts needed to restore runs in Northeastern watersheds. (Calhoun)

- The two federal fisheries services, in concert with the New England states, develop a comprehensive state-federal-international Atlantic salmon plan for New England, giving careful attention to evaluation and restoration of river environments, hatchery production and smolt distribution. (Calhoun)

- Service participation in rebuilding certain major, economically valuable fishery resources to full, self-sustainable productivity. Emphasis on anadromous and Great Lakes resources represented by indigenous, or native, species within their original ranges. Re-creation of harvestable surpluses produced by self-replenishing fish stocks. Irreversible habitat loss will proscribe restoration of some stocks to former productivity, necessitating augmentation by mitigation stocking, in perpetuity. (R&R)

- Establish cooperative restoration goals and targets for depleted fishery resources and determine the level of FWS contribution. The FWS does not view as a federal obligation "enhancement" by artificial means of fishery resources in whose restoration it participated. Costs related to providing hatchery fish for augmentation, creation, and nonmitigation maintenance of fishery resources are properly borne by beneficiaries through the states and tribes. (R&R)

- FWS restoration responsibilities for depleted, interjurisdictional resources are: (R&R)

    - Pacific salmons and steelhead trout.

    - Great Lakes lake trout and contemporary species.

    - Anadromous Atlantic salmon.

    - Anadromous nonsalmonid Atlantic and Gulf of Mexico fishes (e.g. striped bass, shads, herrings, sturgeons).

    - Transboundary intercoastal and estuarine fishes (e.g. red drum, weakfish, and other sciaenids).

- FWS involvement, underwritten by the development agency, must continue for as long as mitigation requirements have to be satisfied, entailing a perpetual need to stock hatchery–produced fish where anadromous runs have been blocked by high dams. There is a corresponding need for continuous evaluation of the performance of both the mitigation product and that of the fisheries that it benefits. (R&R)

- In the specific case of existing de facto mitigation facilities, it is the Department of the Interior and FWS intent to pursue cost-sharing arrangements for their future operation and maintenance with the agencies representing project beneficiaries...with full state and tribal participation, as appropriate. (R&R)

- Assistance is provided through participating tribes and states for maintenance and enhancement of fishery resources in waters on federal land when the FWS is requested to do so and is funded by the respective land management agency. (R&R)

- Defer to states and others the operation of new fish propagation facilities serving mitigation purposes. (R&R)

- Artificial propagation should not be used as a substitute for an aggressive program of habitat restoration or habitat protection. (NFWF)

- The obligation to stock federal fish should end as soon as self-sustaining populations are achieved or it is determined such populations are not possible. The use of non-FWS funding sources and organizations should be considered for covering the costs of annual stocking, if it is to continue. (NFWF)

- Stocking propagated fish in ecosystem management, in restoration of depleted stocks, or for threatened and endangered species should only be done in areas determined to have suitable habitat, adequate food base, and appropriate spawning areas and based on specific analyses and implementation plans, such as endangered species recovery plans. Appropriate inland and marine harvest regimes should be an agreed-upon element of an ecosystem management plan. (NFWF)

- Mitigation hatcheries should be reviewed to determine if original goal is being achieved. If not, determine why and take appropriate corrective action in concert with affected state/tribe. (NFWF)

- No private waters should be stocked with federally produced fish for recreational fishing. (NFWF)

- Enhancement of fish populations beyond natural production levels in order to provide greater recreational opportunities (put-and-take) is not a federal responsibility. Requests for federal hatchery fish to enhance recreational fishing should be accompanied by a willingness to assume the cost of production. (This was not a consensus recommendation.) (NFWF)

- The FWS will aggressively pursue implementation of the Recreational Fishery Resources Conservation Plan and subsequent FWS plan developed under Executive Order 12962, Recreational Fisheries. (SM)

- Where FWS hatchery production is the agreed-upon tool for mitigating impacts, the FWS will continue production until a better tool becomes available, or there is no longer a need to mitigate. (SM)

- The FWS will work with partners, including pursuit of new legislation, to establish adequate and stable funding sources that minimize reliance on public funds appropriated to the FWS for past, present and future mitigation projects. (SM)

- Stakeholders view fish culture support for restoring and/or managing interjurisdictional species as an important FWS role and recommend the FWS provide cultured fish where needed for interjurisdictional fishery restoration and/or management programs. (SM)

- Stakeholders do not place high value on the FWS for urban fishing programs off FWS lands and recommend that urban fishing programs be primarily state and local responsibilities. (SM)

- Beyond FWS activities identified as high priority, the FWS will provide assistance for fish and wildlife management and stock cultured fish on non-FWS federal lands and waters only where requested and reimbursed. However, whether reimbursed or not, such activities will not be considered a priority if they would detract from high-priority FWS activities. (SM)

Threatened, Endangered and Native Species

- Substantial fish cultural operations involving endangered species that are found to be necessary be carried on in new facilities built and operated for that purpose. (Calhoun).

- FWS and NMFS increase emphasis on research and development related to culture of Pacific salmon and steelhead; encourage and participate in state-federal review of existing and proposed projects in this field; encourage and participate in development of a state-federal system for jointly assigning priorities and responsibilities for research and development. (Calhoun)

- The custody of gene pool remnants of fishes with no hope of reestablishment in the wild be assigned to special facilities established for that purpose rather than to hatcheries geared to routine production of game fish. (Calhoun)

- Federal and state governments continue to share responsibility for culture of Pacific salmon and steelhead. (Calhoun)

- Stocking propagated fish in ecosystem management, in restoration of depleted stocks, or for threatened and endangered species should only be done in areas determined to have suitable habitat, adequate food base, and appropriate spawning areas and based on specific analyses and implementation plans, such as endangered species recovery plans. Appropriate inland and marine harvest regimes should be an agreed-upon element of an ecosystem management plan (NFWF)

- Federally produced threatened and endangered species may be stocked in private waters if part of a recovery plan and agreed to by private landowners of waters in question. (NFWF)

- Develop a planning process for captive protection of threatened and endangered species for possible future propagation before a species is listed to assure adequate population numbers are available to maintain heterozygosity in future brood stock (should a decision be made that propagation is needed). (NFWF)

- Develop and use captive propagation techniques for fishes and other aquatic species listed as threatened, endangered, or candidate under the Endangered Species Act, when specifically prescribed in recovery plans. Other techniques that are in accordance with conservation genetic principles and in conjunction with habitat restoration may be approved by the FWS director. (AP)

- All future funding for endangered species work conducted by the FWS Fisheries Program will be requested discretely and not displace funding for work with nonlisted fishes. (SM)

Funding Considerations

- National fish hatchery operations should become a more defined part of the regional FWS budgets. (NFWF)

- Efforts should be made to revisit all mitigation mandates with the intent of having the developing agency underwrite all operational costs, needed maintenance, plus any expenses to correct failed mitigation efforts. (NFWF)

- Following a Department of the Interior Inspector General (IG) review of FWS attempts to recover costs for hatchery operations at national fish hatcheries used to mitigate Bureau of Reclamation projects, the IG recommended:

    -Amending a memorandum of agreement with the Bureau of Reclamation to establish procedures to ensure project beneficiaries are required to pay for reimbursable mitigation costs attributable to the Central Valley Project. (IG)

    -Getting a solicitor's opinion concerning recoverability of expenditures at Coleman Hatchery from 1950-1989, under the present agreement with the Bureau of Reclamation. If recoverable, coordinate with the Bureau of Reclamation to ensure all reimbursable costs are identified and assessed to project beneficiaries. (IG)

    -Obtaining authority to allow the federal government to recover costs in operating the Leavenworth hatcheries complex. Negotiate a new agreement to establish procedures to ensure project beneficiaries are assessed the reimbursable portion of mitigation costs attributable to the Columbia Basin Project. (IG)

- All future funding for endangered species work conducted by the FWS Fisheries Program will be requested discretely and not displace funding for work with nonlisted fishes. (SM)

Discussion of the Roles of and Need for the National Fish Hatchery System's Fish Technology Centers, Fish Health Centers, and the National Brood-Stock Program

Fish Technology Centers

The Fish and Wildlife Service's (FWS) seven fish technology centers were established in 1965 to develop and improve fish culture techniques and to provide assistance and advice about fish culture to national fish hatcheries and to other federal and state agencies, tribes, private aquaculture and, occasionally, other countries. Over time, responsibilities have grown, and areas of specialty have expanded to include technical support for interjurisdictional fisheries, estuarine and riverine fisheries, nonindigenous aquatic nuisance species, threatened and endangered aquatic species, and other high-priority aquatic resource issues.

Today, these fish technology centers provide support to the National Fish Hatchery System (NFHS) with emphasis on assessing the quality, genetic diversity, and post-release survival of captive-reared fish; identifying and reducing detrimental effects of hatchery releases on wild fish; assisting in the restoration of naturally spawning stocks; developing technologies to reduce water consumption and pollution in hatcheries; assembling a data base of genetic fingerprints of many wild fish stocks; developing cryopreservation techniques to safeguard DNA of threatened or endangered species; and developing and improving diets to meet the nutritional needs of captive-reared fish.

The steering committee believes fish technology centers can and should work to refine existing protocols and develop new ones for post-release evaluation, evaluation of the effects of intra- and interstate movement of hatchery-raised fish on wild native species, and the effects and control of exotic diseases, exotic fish and nonindigenous aquatic nuisance species.

Fish Health Centers

The FWS' nine fish health centers work cooperatively with federal, state and tribal fishery managers to detect, identify, document, and control fish pathogens and diseases in hatchery-reared and wild stocks. These centers provide core diagnostics, monitoring, and technical assistance services essential to maintaining healthy fish populations and reducing impacts of fish diseases. They also are developing nonlethal, innovative methods of sampling for disease so that the health of rare, threatened and endangered species can be monitored without sacrificing individual fish. Data from the National Wild Fish Health Survey, prepared by the fish health centers, provide support that is useful in all fish conservation activities.

Brood-Stock Hatcheries

The 13 national fish hatcheries affiliated with the national brood-stock program provide a source of pathogen-free eggs from a variety of distinct strains that are managed to maintain the highest degree of genetic variability. Eggs from the national brood-stock program help fill the needs of FWS, state and tribal fishery management biologists in meeting resource management and fishery objectives. Many of the partners use the products of the FWS brood-stock program for recreational programs to relieve pressure on native stocks.

In exchange, states and tribes often assist the FWS in working on high-priority restoration and recovery programs. All FWS inland trout brood-stock facilities have brood-stock management plans outlining accepted methods and procedures for rearing, spawning, feeding, handling and maintaining genetic variation in brood stocks. The national brood-stock program also cooperates in the national fish strain registry. This venture with the U.S. Geological Survey's Wellsboro Laboratory provides fishery mangers with valuable information about brood-stock performance, genetics, fish health and fish availability for trout, paddlefish, sturgeon and catfish. Work on coolwater fishes and sunfish is underway.

The national brood-stock program is positioned to greatly reduce the potential for diseased or genetically inappropriate fish being released into the nation's most important waters, and that position should be maintained and strengthened.

Discussion of National Fish Hatcheries—Mitigation Funding

A principal issue for the Fish and Wildlife Service (FWS) appears to be one of continuing to adequately fund national fish hatcheries responsible for producing fish for mitigation, while at the same time increasing emphasis on using hatcheries for endangered species recovery and native stock restoration. This was more fully explored in the General Accounting Office Report of June 2000, "National Fish Hatcheries: Authority Needed to Better Align Operations With Priorities."

Thirty-eight national fish hatcheries are currently involved either totally or partially in mitigation as a result of federally funded dams and other developments. Thirteen provide fish as mitigation as specifically identified in an act authorizing a dam (statutory mitigation). Twenty-five provide mitigation fish for developments that did not specifically specify the use of hatcheries in the authorizations (de-facto mitigation). Costs for approximately one-third of these 38 hatcheries are recovered or reimbursed in a variety of ways, as discussed below.

In 1985, the FWS *Statement of Responsibilities and Role* identified the need to have dam beneficiaries (power consumers, water users) pay for the cost of operation and maintenance of mitigation hatcheries. In 1991, the Department of the Interior Office of Inspector General performed an audit of FWS cost recovery and determined that the FWS was not following up on the cost-recovery goal identified in the Statement of Responsibilities and Role.

Subsequently, FWS negotiated an agreement with the Bureau of Reclamation to have the bureau be responsible for funding costs for Coleman National Fish Hatchery in California, and Leavenworth, Entiat, and Winthrop national fish hatcheries in Washington. The bureau recovers these costs from project beneficiaries.

The Mitchell Act of 1938, as amended, provided for hatcheries in the Lower Columbia River. The act brought the states and FWS into partnership through the Lower Columbia River Fishery Development Program. The program provides federal funding through the National Marine Fisheries Service (NMFS) to Oregon, Washington, and Idaho and to FWS to support hatchery operations related to water development projects on the lower Columbia River. Four national fish hatcheries receive Mitchell Act funds: Little White Salmon, Willard, Carson and Spring Creek, appropriated through the Department of Commerce. However, funding over the last several years has not been adequate, with maintenance being deferred.

The Water Resource Development Act of 1976 authorized the Lower Snake River Compensation Plan (LSRCP) to compensate for losses due to federal dams. Twenty-seven hatcheries resulted in the Lower Snake. The LSRCP gives FWS responsibility for operating Dworshak and Hagerman national fish hatcheries in Idaho. Costs to FWS are reimbursed annually through the U.S. Treasury by Bonneville Power Administration (BPA). BPA recovers costs through ratepayer revenues.

The Northwest Power Planning and Conservation Act directed Oregon, Washington, Idaho and Montana to balance use of the Columbia River for power with fish and wildlife. It directed BPA to pay for fisheries offsets from construction of Hungry Horse, Kerr and Big Fork dams and to recover those costs from electric ratepayers. The Creston National Fish Hatchery in Montana provides fish production to mitigate for Kerr Dam.

The Colorado River Storage Act of 1956 authorized the Secretary of the Interior to plan, construct, operate and maintain facilities to mitigate losses due to over 20 water storage projects on the Colorado River. Jones Hole National Fish Hatchery in Utah and Hotchkiss National Fish Hatchery in Colorado receive direct funding as a result.

The remaining hatcheries involved with fishery mitigation are funded through regular hatchery appropriations. This funding is augmented by a variety of trade-off and sharing arrangements with the states. Six of the 17 hatcheries are in the Southeast, with annual costs of about $2.3 million. FWS estimates that $4.5 million annually would be necessary to fully recover costs from project beneficiaries, not including the $5.8 million maintenance backlog. Information from the FWS' Southeast Region, based in part on the American Sportfishing Association's publication "The Economic Importance of Sport Fishing," indicates an annual economic benefit of over $400 million from those six hatcheries.

The 1995 "SFBPC Report to FWS on Cost-Saving Recommendations for the FY 1997 Fisheries Program" reaffirmed that the cost of mitigation should be borne by federal project beneficiaries and recommended FWS seek congressional authorization for fee collection through user-pay.

As part of the FWS 1996-97 stakeholder process, stakeholders indicated that they were willing to work in partnership with FWS to strengthen the role of the Fisheries Program, including national fish hatcheries. The FWS summary of these national stakeholder meetings states "...stakeholders highly value Service responsibilities for mitigation," and feel strongly that when national fish hatchery fish are the agreed-upon mitigation action, FWS should not attempt to abrogate that responsibility. Stakeholders encouraged the FWS and states to undertake an effort to obtain reimbursement from project beneficiaries or development agencies to establish adequate and stable funding sources. This included the suggestion that, in some cases, an entity other than the FWS might assume the mitigation responsibility.